The Accountability Advantage

5 Proven Steps to Build a Culture of
Trust, Ownership, and Results

Dr. Quendrida Whitmore

great ideas
publishing

Great Ideas Publishing

ISBN-13: 979-8-9926697-6-3 (print)
ISBN-13: 979-8-9926697-7-0 (ebook)
ISBN-13: 979-8-9926697-8-7 (audiobook)

Library of Congress Control Number: 2025908048

Published by Great Ideas Publishing
Bloomington, MN
greatideaspublishing.com

Contents

Introduction: Why Accountability Changes Everything

The Myth of Accountability

What comes to mind when you hear the word accountability?

Most leaders pause. Some bristle. Others immediately think of awkward conversations, performance reviews, or being "called out" in a meeting. For many leaders, the word feels heavy, like consequences, correction, or termination. It's something you do when someone drops the ball.

But here's the truth: *accountability isn't about blame*. It's about the belief that people want to own their work, want to contribute at a high level, and want to be trusted. It's about equipping them to rise, take ownership, and drive results because they choose to, not because they fear the alternative.

Reframing Accountability as Empowerment

Accountability happens at the intersection of ownership, clarity, and support.

> **Accountability = ownership + clarity + support**

Accountability is *creating alignment and building trust*, not just enforcing expectations.

Accountability happens when everyone knows what they own, why it matters, how they'll be supported in getting there, and the impact when it doesn't happen.

It's not about control. It's about clarity, trust, and alignment. These three ingredients transform well-meaning individuals into a high-performing team.

> **Accountability Is NOT:**
> **Blame | Micromanagement | Control | Fear-based leadership**

When accountability is built into the culture, team members don't wait to be told what to do; they anticipate, act, and deliver. Leaders don't chase updates; they focus on vision and growth. People *stop hiding and start rising.*

The Avengers Effect

Think of your team like a superhero squad, not one leader doing everything, but a group of talented individuals, each with unique powers, working toward a shared mission. That's the goal.

Now imagine if those heroes didn't trust each other. If no one knew the mission. If one was fighting aliens, another was stuck in traffic, and two were arguing over whose job it was to save the city and who would get credit.

That's what a *lack of accountability* feels like.

But when there's clarity, shared purpose, core roles, and ownership, it's a different story. Each person owns their lane. They back each other up because it's about the team's success, not individual greatness. They adapt in real-time. And when the pressure's on, they rise together!

Why This Matters Now

- You are tired of micromanaging.

- Potential is high on your team, but results are inconsistent.

- You're putting out fires instead of building something lasting.

- Culture is friendly but not high-performing.

- You want to spend more time leading and less time chasing.

Accountability is the lever. When it's clear, consistent, and modeled at the top, it becomes the invisible force that turns individuals into owners and teams into high-performing superheroes.

What's to Come

In this book, you'll learn how to build a culture of accountability using five proven steps, starting with yourself and scaling to your entire team. You'll explore how to lead with clarity, consistency, and courage and finally create the kind of culture that performs even when you're not in the room.

In the next chapters, you'll learn how to:

- Build accountability starting with *YOU*

- Clarify expectations so people know what winning looks like

- Develop the team by changing your leadership style based on what's needed

- Create routines that lock in follow-through

- Have conversations that drive ownership, not defensiveness

You'll walk away with tools, examples, and strategies to turn your team into the kind of high-performing force that delivers, even when you're not in the room.

The Accountability Advantage Journal

Before you dive into the next chapter, I want to invite you to do something simple but powerful: grab a notebook or journal.

Label it your Accountability Advantage Journal, digital or paper, doesn't matter. What matters is that you commit to using it. *One note: you do remember what you write better than what you type, but I won't push this point.* Digital or paper, whichever you prefer.

Why a journal?

Because this isn't just a book to read. It's a book to work. To wrestle with. To respond to.

Throughout each chapter, you'll find:

- Reflection questions to challenge how you lead

- Prompts to help you align intention with action

- Practical tips and tools to take back to your team

- Stories that may mirror your own leadership moments

The best way to make this more than information, and turn it into transformation, is to capture what's coming up for you in each chapter. *As you read*, write down:

- What hits. What stings. What excites you.

- That action you know you need to take.

- The one sentence you need to revisit tomorrow.

This isn't about perfection. It's about presence. Show up to this work with curiosity and courage, and bring your notebook along.

Leadership isn't just built in meetings or metrics. It's built in moments like this, when you slow down, reflect, and choose to lead with intention. As Schön said, learning happens in reflection.[1] If you keep moving without pausing to reflect, you may miss the lesson.

Let's get to it!

Dr. Quendrida Whitmore

---

1. Schön, D. A. (1983). *The reflective practitioner: How professionals think in action*. Basic Books.

PART I

ACCOUNTABILITY
MINDSET

Chapter One

Accountability Is Not What You Think

The "Blame Trap": Why Most People Misunderstand Accountability

For many teams, "accountability" is code for:

- Who messed up?

- Who's getting written up?

- Who's not doing their job?

- Who's getting fired?

That mindset doesn't foster responsibility; it fuels defensiveness and avoidance. It locks leaders in a reactive loop where accountability only shows up after something has already gone wrong.

Real accountability doesn't begin with failure. It starts with clarity. Let me say that again, *real accountability doesn't begin with failure. It starts with clarity.*

It's not about catching someone in the act; it's about *inviting team members into ownership* from the start.

I have been a leader for over two decades and heard many myths about accountability. Things people tell themselves and each other that keep them stuck in a cycle of restating expectations and never moving the team or results forward. Here are some of the most common myths about accountability that I have heard, as well as the truth, if you choose to accept it.[1234567]

COMMON MYTHS TO BUST

MYTH	TRUTH
Accountability = Punishment	Accountability = Ownership + Support
Accountability is just about hitting goals	Accountability is about how people show up and contribute
Leaders are solely responsible for holding others accountable	Leaders model and create a culture of accountability, where individuals hold themselves and each other accountable
You either have accountability, or you don't	Accountability can be developed intentionally

Now that we've cleared up what accountability is not, let's talk about what it truly is.

A Better Definition: What Accountability Really Is

Let's define it clearly and simply:

As Michael Timms points out, "Accountability is taking ownership of results and working to improve future results".[8]

I remember the first time I saw the "What is Accountability" video from Michael Timms, and I said out loud, "That's it!" We are over-complicating accountability. His simple definition stripped away the heaviness of the word and made space for its power and possibility. It was a reset, one that made me realize we've been talking about accountability like it's a punishment when, really, it's a pathway.

With this definition, your team and audience can finally get excited about accountability, because it stops being a bad word. And when it stops being something to fear, it becomes something to embrace.

Accountability becomes ownership.

- It becomes clarity.

- It becomes momentum, growth, and shared pride.

- It becomes the culture you've been trying to build, one where people step up, not shut down.

Let's dive deeper into what accountability actually looks and feels like when it's done well, and how to create it from the inside out.

Accountability is not about being perfect; it's about being *engaged, aligned, and responsible.*[9][10][11][12][13] It's about:

- Knowing what success looks like.

- Owning your role and achieving results.

- Communicating openly when support is needed.

- Following through with consistency.

- Free flow of feedback (both positive and constructive) from all on the team.

When accountability is defined this way, it becomes an act of leadership, not discipline.

The Impact of True Accountability on Team Culture

What happens when everyone owns their role?

I have heard many people say, "Stay in your lane", but I like saying, "Own your role". When you think about it, staying in your lane can be perceived as you do your thing, and I'll do mine. That doesn't inspire collaboration, aligned goals, or teamwork.

> 📢
>
> **Coach Quen Says: "Owning your role means showing up for the good of the project, the team, and the results."**

Imagine an orchestra where the horn section stayed out late the night before practice and didn't have their parts down. They didn't own their role. When the orchestra plays, you will hear them, not in a good way. They won't be aligned or in step with the rest of the team. But when everyone in an orchestra owns their role, beautiful music is played, and the audience is in awe of what can be accomplished. This is no different from your team.

When everyone owns their role:

- Projects move forward faster.

- Communication gets clearer.

- Trust deepens.

- Leaders lead instead of chase, remind, or rescue.

- High-performers stay because expectations are fair and enforced.

- Individuals, teams, and organizations win!

Accountability doesn't limit your team; it frees them.

Accountability creates *psychological safety* because people know what's expected and where they stand. It builds mutual respect because no one is dragging the rest of the team down. And it unlocks performance because everyone is rowing in the same direction (or, in our metaphor, assembling with clarity like the Avengers).

There is one big part of accountability that we have to address. This concept is that accountability starts with you. Many love to start accountability by pointing the finger at others saying, "They need to be held accountable". Because of this, I built a model to clearly demonstrate accountability actually starts with *YOU!*

Introducing the Accountability Culture Model: Self → Team → Others

Why start with self-accountability?

Because if leaders don't walk the talk, nothing else sticks.

I built this model when I started working with an organization that needed help creating a culture of ownership and accountability. When I was doing my introductory interviews, with the goal of learning about the culture, I must have spoken to almost 50 people.

Interestingly, I heard a common thread. Almost every person I spoke to said, "they need to be held accountable". Even though they were not physically pointing a finger, I could feel, sense, and understand that they were pointing a finger at everyone else but themselves. Not one person started with, "This is what I need to do differently".

I reflected on the first steps to moving this culture which were creating a common language and definition of accountability that didn't begin with others.

Because of this experience, I built the Accountability Culture Model: Self → Team → Others. This model demonstrates how accountability starts with self and then moves to your team before you get to others. In this diagram, they all overlap, creating a culture of accountability.

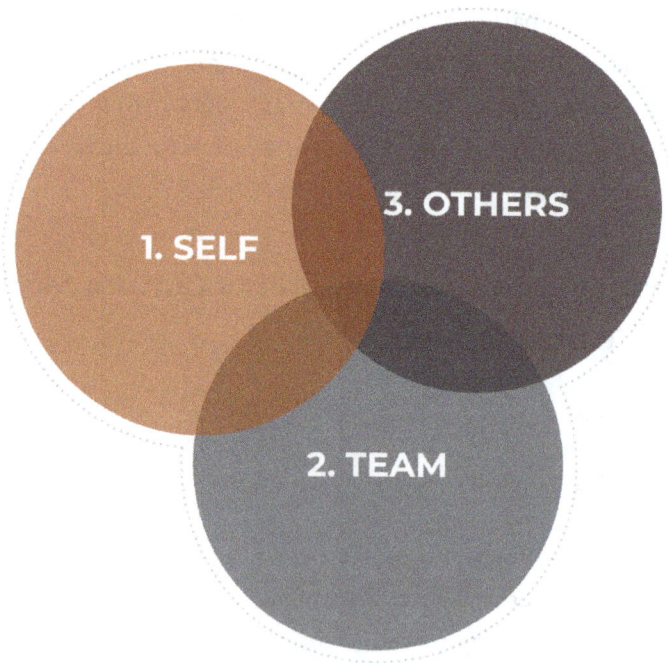

1. Self-Accountability

Understanding your role, responsibility, and ownership is the first step of accountability.

2. Team Accountability

Leader and team (including peer-to-peer) follow-up. Coaching, directing, follow-up, and follow-through are all part of team accountability.

3. Others' Accountability

Driven through collaboration. Identifying each person's role, setting follow-up timelines, and defining success are vital to holding others accountable.

Building and teaching this model gave me the clarity and language I needed to start shifting the conversation and the culture from blame to ownership.

It allowed everyone in the organization to align on what accountability actually means, where it begins, and what it looks like in action.

That's where the change started, not with policy but with perspective.

You can't build a culture of accountability until each person owns their stuff. I call this "owning your crazy". We all have a little crazy, let's admit it. You must be able to look inward at what you need to do differently before you can look at your team or others. Because of this, you won't be surprised that many of the tips and suggested actions in this book are about you first.

Closing

I encourage you to think about if you are trapped in myths about accountability that are causing you to be stuck in inaction. Accountability is tough if you try to start with others. That is precisely why you have to start with you first. By the end of this book, you will have a road map to get you unstuck and turn you into an accountability master.

Next, let's talk about how culture is created. The hard truth is this: it's always being created, whether you're intentional or not. The good news is you can be intentional.

---

1. Evans, M. (2017). *Achieve with accountability: Ignite engagement, ownership, perseverance, alignment, and change.* Sound Wisdom.

2. Molinaro, V. (2020). *Accountable leaders: Inspire a culture where everyone steps up, takes ownership, and delivers results.* Wiley.

3. Reeves, D. B. (2004). *Accountability for learning: How teachers and school leaders can take charge.* ASCD.

4. Green, J. (2011). *Education, professionalism, and the quest for accountability: Hitting the target but missing the point.* Routledge.

5. Melo, P. N., Martins, A., & Pereira, M. (2020). The relationship between leadership and accountability: A review and synthesis of the research. *International Journal of Business Excellence.*

6. Brinkerhoff, D. W. (2001). *Taking account of accountability: A conceptual overview and strategic options.* U.S. Agency for International Development.

7. Newell, P., & Bellour, S. (2002). *Mapping accountability: Origins, contexts and implications for development.* Institute of Development Studies.

8. Timms, Michael. "What is Accountability?" *YouTube,* 6 September 2021

9. Balogun, O., & Zaghmout, B. (2024). *Exploring leadership excellence and accountability in organisational dynamics: A comprehensive analysis in Nigeria.* African Journal of Environmental Science and Development.

10. Ciuta, S. (n.d.). *Leadership unleashed: Inspiring excellence.* Independently published.

11. Evans, M. (2017). *Achieve with accountability: Ignite engagement, ownership, perseverance, alignment, and change.* Sound Wisdom.

12. Jenkins, J., Lock, L., & Lock, M. A. (2018). Leadership—A critical bridge to accountability. *International Journal of Educational Leadership Preparation, 13*(1).

13. Molinaro, V. (2020). *Accountable leaders: Inspire a culture where everyone steps up, takes ownership, and delivers results.* Wiley.

Chapter Two

Culture Is Always Being Created

Leadership Creates Culture — Whether You Mean To or Not

Coach Quen Says - "Culture is always being created. The only question is whether you're doing it on purpose."

Most leaders think of culture as something built during retreats or printed on company values posters. But culture isn't built in all-hands meetings. It's created in moments.

- When someone misses a deadline, and there's no follow-up

- When a tough issue is avoided to "keep the peace"

- When a leader praises effort but ignores inconsistency

- When team norms aren't aligned with actual behaviors

- When more work is given to the top performers because "it will get done"

These small, everyday moments shape culture, whether you intend them to or not.

Accidental Culture vs. Intentional Culture

Let's define the two.[123456789]

ACCIDENTAL CULTURE	INTENTIONAL CULTURE
Built by habits and assumptions	Built by design and example
Inconsistent responses to behavior	Clear expectations and norms
Fear, silence, or confusion	Trust, feedback, and alignment
Leaders say one thing but do another	Leaders model what they expect

Is your current culture happening by design or by default?

📖 Storytime: Culture Is Always Being Created

I once worked with a leader who was under tremendous pressure to deliver results. The stakes were high, and the heat was on. To his credit, he often asked for his team's input, "What do you think?" "Any ideas?". But, when people spoke up, things would quickly take a turn.

If he didn't like the idea, he'd shoot it down, not just directly but sharply, often using colorful language and sarcasm that left people feeling small. You would watch it happen in real-time: people would shut down, eyes would drop, and the energy would drain from the room.

He didn't understand why the team stopped offering ideas. Why no one gave him feedback. Why conversations in meetings became surface-level and safe.

But the reason was simple: a culture of silence had taken root.

No one declared it. No memo was sent. But the team learned, quickly, that speaking up wasn't worth the risk.

Turnover rose. Trust declined. And that leader, unknowingly, built the very culture he was frustrated by.

Lesson Learned: Culture is always being created. Whether intentionally or not, people adapt to what gets rewarded, avoided, and tolerated. And more than anything else, they adapt to how leaders show up.

What Gets Reinforced, Repeats

Culture isn't what you say; it's what you *tolerate, reward, and reinforce.*

- If you consistently ignore late work, it becomes normal.

- If you celebrate ownership, it becomes contagious.

Leaders shape team norms through:

- What they follow up on

- What they recognize

- What they let slide

- What they model in everyday behavior

These signals, even if subtle, tell your team what's acceptable, what's expected, and what matters.

When I shifted from corporate to the field team, I realized how important repetition was. When you see your team every day, you get many instances in a week to correct any miscommunication. In the field, you don't see your leaders every day, so the communication has to be precise and specific.

Leaders say a lot in a day, a week, and a month. Repetition helps the team understand what the true priority is when they are deciding what to act on. What gets reinforced and repeated gets the attention. If you are not repeating the important stuff, your team is most likely picking what *they* think is most important, which may not be aligned with your expectations. This personal selection is not from poor intentions; it's from lack of clarity from you, the leader.

Be the leader who brings clarity.

It's the difference between a team moving in the same direction or everyone moving toward their own version of the goal.

Your Team Is Watching (and Mirroring)

Whether you realize it or not, your team is always scanning.[101112]

- Do you follow through?

- Do you make excuses or own mistakes?

- Do you give feedback early or wait until things go wrong?

- Do you speak with clarity or leave things vague?

Leadership behavior sets the *cultural tone and performance bar* for the entire team.

📖 Storytime: They're Always Watching

I was leading a team of district managers, and we were in the middle of a quarterly strategy meeting, talking about priorities, people, and performance. This was pre-COVID, so most of our regular team meetings were over the phone. We'd jump on weekly conference calls, and while I made monthly market visits, the face-to-face moments were meaningful but not frequent.

That's what made what happened next so surprising.

We were having a light moment as a team, joking about things I "always do", you know, those leadership quirks people love to point out. Someone mentioned my tendency to say "right" all the time. Another mentioned a phrase I use when I'm ready to pivot the conversation.

Then one of the district leaders chimed in:
"No, that's not it. You know what she always does? She pushes her glasses up and tilts her head to the side; that's when she's about to challenge something or isn't quite sold."

The room laughed. I froze.

Partly because I didn't even realize I did that.
And partly because, with only limited in-person time together, she had picked up on a micro-movement I didn't know I was making.

She was watching me like a hawk.
Not in a negative way, but in the way people watch leaders for cultural cues.

Approval. Disapproval. Agreement. Doubt.
It was all being read through tone, posture, facial expression, even glasses.

That moment reminded me in a visceral way: Culture is always being created.

Not just in what you say, but in how you say it.
Not just in what you declare, but in what you display.

Whether you're on a big stage or a small Zoom box, your team is watching.
Not because they're judging but because they're trying to figure out how to belong, how to win, and how to lead others themselves.

What are the subtle signals your body language or tone might be sending, even when you're not speaking?

Lesson Learned: Your team takes their cultural cues from your words, your tone, your body language, and your consistency. Every interaction is a signal. Every moment is a message.

If you're inconsistent, the team is unsure. If *you're over-functioning, the team under-functions.* If you model accountability, the team starts to mirror it. They are paying attention.

Coach Quen Says: "Intentional culture is created when words and actions are in alignment."

When words and actions align, trust grows. When they don't, confusion and frustration set in.

A leader's job is to guide the "right" culture, to ensure that what's said, seen, and supported is aligned. And that starts with modeling, not mandating, accountability.

As an executive leadership coach, I often give clients reflection questions and homework to challenge them to pause, reflect, and take action. Here's your first reflection and challenge.

The Culture Audit: A Quick Gut Check

 Leadership Reflection:

1. What's one behavior I've been tolerating that contradicts the culture I want?

2. What's one behavior I've been modeling that strengthens it?

3. What do I *assume* my team knows about our culture but they haven't said out loud?

This short reflective pause creates the mindset shift needed to lead with intention in the next chapter.

Leadership Challenge:

Culture isn't in an HR deck. It's in the way your team behaves when you're not in the room.

Are you leading culture or letting it happen to you?
Ask your boss, one peer, and two direct reports: "What do you perceive our team culture to be?"

In the next chapter, we begin the 5-Step Framework, starting where all accountability begins: you. We'll explore how your self-awareness, strengths, blind spots, and behavior patterns shape everything else.

The 5-Step Accountability Advantage Framework takes you through multiple steps to help build a culture of accountability. Here's the model we will be moving through.

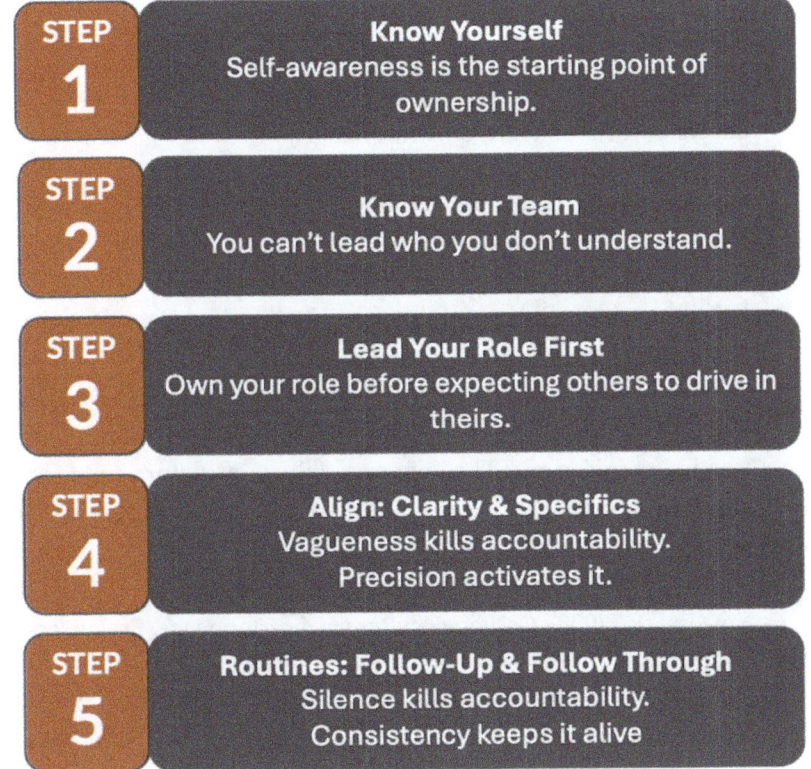

Closing

The 5-Step Accountability Framework will help you move from a haphazard culture, that may or may not be what you want or what the business needs, to an intentional culture with alignment, clarity, and accountability.

Remember, you are the leader. Your team watches for cues, behaviors, and decisions that reflect your words. If those things don't align, the team notices and follows suit.

---

1. Cooper, M. D. (2000). Towards a model of safety culture. Safety Science, 36(2), 111-136.

2. Driskill, G. (2018). Organizational culture in action: A cultural analysis workbook (3rd ed.). Routledge.

3. Fairholm, G. W. (1994). *Leadership and the culture of trust*. Praeger.

4. Hermalin, B. E. (2013). Leadership and corporate culture. In R. Gibbons & J. Roberts (Eds.), *The Handbook of Organizational Economics* (pp. 430-478). Princeton University Press.

5. Hoogervorst, J., & van der Flier, H. (2004). Implicit communication in organisations: The impact of culture, structure and management practices on employee behaviour. *Journal of Managerial Psychology, 19*(3), 245-267.

6. Kotter, J. P. (2008). *Corporate culture and performance*. Free Press.

7. Nguyen, H. N., & Mohamed, S. (2011). Leadership behaviors, organizational culture and knowledge management practices: An empirical investigation. *Journal of Management Development, 30*(2), 206-221.

8. Reason, J. (1998). Achieving a safe culture: theory and practice. *Work & Stress, 12*(3), 293-306.

9. Tsui, A. S., Zhang, Z. X., Wang, H., Xin, K. R., & Wu, J. B. (2006). Unpacking the relationship between CEO leadership behavior and organizational culture. *The Leadership Quarterly, 17*(2), 113–137.

10. Hunter, E. M., Neubert, M. J., Perry, S. J., & Witt, L. A. (2013). Servant leaders inspire servant followers: Antecedents and outcomes for employees and the organization. *The Leadership Quarterly, 24*(2), 316–331.

11. Athanasopoulou, A., & Moss-Cowan, A. (2018). Claiming the corner office: Female CEO careers and implications for leadership development. *Human Resource Management, 57*(2), 617–641.

12. Hughes, B. C. (2022). Examining toxic leadership: An integrated framework for organizational recovery. *Journal of Business and Management, 28*(1).

PART II

THE 5-STEP
FRAMEWORK

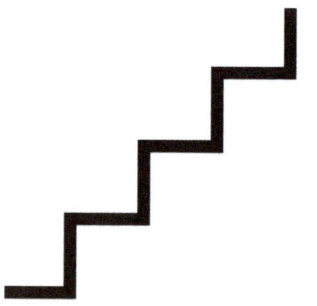

Chapter Three

Know Yourself: Lead from Self-Awareness (Step 1)

Why Accountability Begins With You

I'm a values-based coach, and I believe self-awareness is the foundation of effective leadership.

You can't expect what you don't model. If you want a team that:

- Owns their outcomes

- Admits mistakes

- Seeks feedback

- Pushes for growth

...then, you have to go first. Tag, you're it.

Accountability isn't a message you deliver. It's a mindset you live and model, every day.

📖 Storytime: Self-Awareness and the Trust Gap

I once worked for a leader who talked a lot about being "people first." She'd say it often, "Quendrida, you know me, I'm people first."

But every decision, every conversation, every meeting...was results first. The message underneath was always about numbers, output, performance.

Now, don't get me wrong, I can get behind results. That wasn't the issue. What bothered me wasn't her focus; it was the disconnect between who she was and how she spoke about herself.

She didn't seem to see it. And that's what made it hard to trust her.

Trust doesn't start with charisma or credentials. It starts with self-awareness. It starts when a leader knows who they are, owns it, and leads from a place of honesty and alignment.

Because she didn't seem to know herself, I never felt safe fully being myself either. I led from a place of uncertainty, always second-guessing, always scanning for cues. Not from confidence. Not from clarity. Not from growth.

Lesson Learned: The cost of low self-awareness in leadership is trust. The gap between *who you are* and *who you say you are* is where trust either lives or dies.

Self-Awareness is the Starting Point of Ownership

Leadership is about knowing how your energy, words, and actions shape the room.[123456]

Self-awareness means:

- Understanding your strengths and how you use them (or overuse them)

- Recognizing your emotional triggers and recovery patterns

- Knowing how others perceive you, not just how you intend to show up

- Seeing the gap between what you say and how you behave, and that it matters

Without this, you lead from emotion and on autopilot. Simon Sinek calls this the "lazy leader".[7]

A lazy leader rarely builds a culture of accountability. The lazy leader shows up and lets things happen. They don't inspire the team, they direct the team. They don't watch for understanding and buy-in, they say their part and then move on. They lean on their title for why people should do things, not on alignment, commitment, and engagement.

Don't be a lazy leader; be a leader who develops, empowers, and motivates the team to reach their full potential.

This is a leadership mindset. Someone who understands their role is to get greatness out of the team. You can only do this with self-awareness first. Here's a grid to help you identify where you are and the impact of the behavior.

THE LEADERSHIP MINDSET & SELF-AWARENESS GRID

Self-Awareness	Behavior	Impact
Unaware & Reactive	Avoids feedback, leads emotionally	Inconsistent and confusing
Self-Aware but Insecure	Knows but hides from it and doesn't admit mistakes	Missed influence and trust or misuses influence and blames
Aware & Accountable	Owns mistakes, invites growth	Models culture, builds credibility

Where do you currently fall? Where do you want to be?

Strengths, Triggers & Overuse

Sometimes, your biggest leadership strength becomes your biggest risk. When strengths are overused…

- Clarity becomes control

- Confidence becomes dominance

- Empathy becomes avoidance

- Urgency becomes pressure

The authors Kaiser, Kaplan, and Overfield call this Lopsided Leadership.[8] They say lopsided leadership is when you are not balanced, demonstrate little self-awareness, and negatively impact the performance of you and the team.

When you lean only on your strengths, regardless of what the situation calls for, this is when overuse happens.

These authors say it can be detrimental to the team and your leadership. By understanding how you overuse your strength, you can better manage your emotions, understand what triggers you, and plan to be balanced.

⊘ *Example:*

I am a structured leader. I love planning, aligning the team, and accomplishing our goals. When my plans don't pay off the way I expected them to, my natural tendency is to go to my strength and do more planning, whether that's what is called for or not. This additional planning often leaves curiosity behind, does not include collaboration, and is me trying to get control of the runaway train.

Let's be clear. This is an overuse!

What I should do is get curious, collaborate, and lean on the team and peers for ideas and solutions. We all comfort ourselves by going to our strengths when we are stressed or triggered. The key is to understand when you overuse your strengths and then shift to be balanced instead of lopsided.

Do you know what overuse looks like in your leadership?

≈ **Leadership Reflection:**

- What's one strength I might be overusing?

- What are my leadership "tells" when stressed?

- What do people say about me when I'm not in the room?

- What patterns am I ready to shift?

Values & Vision Check-In

Self-aware leaders lead from their values, not just their profits. You can't ask others to commit to excellence if you haven't defined what it means for you.

If you're living authentically, your values show up every day and everywhere. My number one value is justice, and I live it every day. I build inclusive teams, and when I perceive unfair systems or behaviors, I take action to correct them.

Most of the time, justice is a great thing, but sometimes....it goes awry. A great example of this is when I'm driving on the highway. If the lane is ending and everyone receives ample notice, there is no way you're getting in front of me at the last minute.

That is not fair!

Instead, I speed up and ride the bumper in front of me till the person gets behind me. Yes, this is how I behave as a grown woman; I have to own my crazy. But wait, it gets worse.

Research shows that zipper merging, also known as late merging, moves traffic faster. So, do we see how I'm overusing my strength? Even in light of data and research, I go to justice and fairness as my values, even if they oppose the data.

What I know about values is that when you are most happy, you are usually living your values and thriving. When you feel most invalidated or disrespected, someone is usually stomping on your values. Values are where your motivations and behaviors are born. Once you understand your values, things become clear. You better understand your leadership and your why. This is an essential part of self-awareness.

△ Leadership Challenge: Values Clarity

- List your top 3 personal leadership values.

- Define what "success" looks like when you're living those values.

- Reflect on where your behavior is aligned, overused, or out of sync.

Go to the Bonus Downloads chapter to leverage this exercise.

Feedback: The Mirror You Need Most

When I was a retail buyer everything I bought was gold, according to me. Thank goodness I had a partner with data to tell me, "Quendrida, that's horrible; put it down". Sometimes, the most important thing we need is a mirror. Someone ready and able to give you honest, constructive feedback to help you, the team, and the business.[9101112]

Self-awareness is incomplete without feedback. Leaders need:

- Peers who will speak the truth

- A coach, mentor, or trusted colleague

- Family and friends can be extremely helpful

We all need regular reflection and feedback loops. *Ask: "What is it like to be led by me?"* That's a scary question, but a transformational one, if you are ready to listen.

Encourage building feedback into leadership routines (e.g., quarterly check-ins, anonymous pulse, leadership 360s, etc.). Understanding how you are perceived as a leader is vital to your self-awareness journey.

One goal should be to receive feedback continuously and through informal channels. As you work to build a culture of accountability, it may be necessary to start with more formal feedback processes to encourage honesty and candor from peers and team members and then work your way to the informal feedback loop.

It's important to note that if you don't listen and apply the formal feedback, you will not build a culture where informal feedback is given.

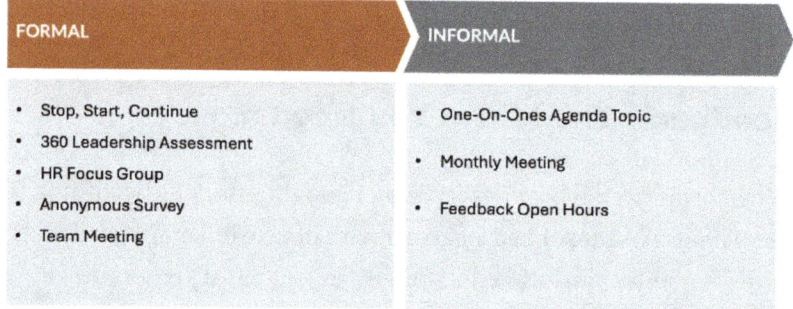

FORMAL	INFORMAL
• Stop, Start, Continue	• One-On-Ones Agenda Topic
• 360 Leadership Assessment	• Monthly Meeting
• HR Focus Group	• Feedback Open Hours
• Anonymous Survey	
• Team Meeting	

When was the last time you asked for or received feedback and applied it to your development?

The Leadership Ripple Effect

Remember, your team is always watching; you must demonstrate that you are a self-aware, engaged leader who drives for authenticity and trust in your culture.

You're always modeling. Always. Every leader casts a ripple:

- If you own your growth, others will.

- If you deflect or delay feedback, they will, too.

- If you get better, so will your team.

You set the standard. You are the tone. You are the first line of culture.

Closing

Remember, you are the key to the culture you want. Knowing yourself is vital to the process of building an accountability culture.

☼ Leadership Reflection:

- What's one leadership habit I want to shift starting this week?

- How do I live my values in the workplace?

- What feedback do I need, and who will I ask?

Reinforce the mindset: *Self-awareness isn't weakness; it's leadership maturity.*

Now that you've looked inward, it's time to look outward, at your team. Because, you can't lead who you don't understand.

---

1. Antonopoulou, H. (2024). *The value of emotional intelligence: Self-awareness, self-regulation, motivation, and empathy as key components.* Semantic Scholar.

2. Bratton, V. K., Dodd, N. G., & Brown, F. W. (2011). The impact of emotional intelligence on accuracy of self-awareness and leadership performance. *Leadership & Organization Development Journal, 32*(2), 127–149.

3. Chon, D. (2022). *Understanding ourselves and organizational leadership: Theory, instrument development, and empirical investigations of self-awareness* [Doctoral dissertation, Duke University]. DukeSpace.

4. Fannon, D. (2018). *The relationship between emotional intelligence and leadership style in educational leaders* [Doctoral dissertation, Pepperdine University]. Pepperdine Digital Commons.

5. Hartung, P. (2020). *The impact of self-awareness on leadership behavior.* Econstor.

6. Showry, M., & Manasa, K. V. L. (2014). Self-awareness: Key to effective leadership. *The IUP Journal of Soft Skills, 8*(1), 15–26.

7. Sinek, S. (2017, October 6). *Rules are for lazy leaders* [Video]. YouTube.

8. Kaiser, R. B., Kaplan, R. E., & Overfield, D. V. (2013). *Fear your strengths: What you are best at could be your biggest problem.* Berrett-Koehler Publishers.

9. McCauley, C. D., & Brutus, S. (2019). Feedback for leadership development. In D. V. Day (Ed.), *The Oxford Handbook of Leadership Development* (pp. 135–154). Oxford University Press.

10. Poon, R. (2023). *Exploring what essential elements are needed for ongoing performance feedback* [Doctoral dissertation, California State University]. ProQuest Dissertations Publishing.

11. Stephenson, L. R. (2025). *The revival: The impact of scaled leadership development on knowledge, team cohesion, and confidence* [Doctoral dissertation, Pepperdine University]. ProQuest Dissertations Publishing.

12. Van Coller-Peter, S., & Burger, Z. (2019). A guiding framework for multi-stakeholder contracting in executive coaching. *SA Journal of Human Resource Management, 17*(1), a1114.

Chapter Four

Know Your Team: Build Belonging & Trust (Step 2)

You can't lead who you don't understand.

Self-awareness is the first step. But leadership isn't complete until it cascades throughout the team. Great leaders don't just manage tasks, they lead individuals by seeing who they are, not just what they do.

According to Hodges and Park, Belonging is a basic human need. When people feel seen, heard, and valued, they show up differently.[1]

They take more risks, contribute ideas, know the team has their back, and feel safe enough to be honest, even when it's hard. That's the foundation of *psychological safety*; without it, accountability doesn't stick.

What Belonging Looks Like

Belonging at work doesn't mean everyone has to agree on everything or even be best friends. I may not want to have dinner with you after work, but I can still respect and value what you bring to the team. Belonging means:

- People feel safe being honest.

- Differences are respected.

- Feedback is a two-way street.

- Contribution is recognized, not just completion.

A team that feels safe and valued is far more likely to:

- Own their results

- Admit when they're stuck

- Support one another under pressure

- Listen to ideas and feedback

People perform at their best when they feel like they matter. That's not softness, that's science.

Here's a Competency Risk grid to help you identify the core competencies, what the team needs, and the risk if the specific driver is absent. This simple grid will help you decode team motivation.

COMPETENCY RISK GRID

Core Competency	What They Need to Feel	Accountability Risk If Absent
Trust	"I'm safe to be honest"	Silence or avoidance
Value	"I matter to the mission"	Disengagement
Clarity	"I know what's expected"	Confusion
Support	"I'm not alone in this"	Blame or burnout
Inclusion	"I don't need to mask who I am"	Low innovation, low retention

Leaders can't guess if someone feels like they belong; they need to ask, observe, and adapt.

Another tool you can leverage to assess ownership and your next move is the ownership grid.

The Ownership Grid

To build a culture of trust and ownership, you have to meet people where they are. Not everyone is motivated the same way, and not everyone needs the same kind of support.

Here's an Ownership Grid that you can leverage to help you identify your leadership move.

OWNERSHIP GRID

Level of Trust	Level of Ownership	What It Looks Like	Leadership Move
Low Trust, Low Ownership	Disengaged	Avoids responsibility, unclear on expectations	Build safety, reset expectations
Low Trust, High Ownership	Lone Wolf	Does their job but stays guarded	Build connection, show value
High Trust, Low Ownership	Drifter	Likes the team, lacks follow-through	Add clarity, coach on standards
High Trust, High Ownership	Accountable Partner	Takes initiative, holds others accountable	Empower, develop, recognize

Your goal? Move people toward the bottom-left corner of high trust, high ownership.

Belonging and Empowerment Leads to Resilience and Retention

When people feel safe, they know they are not alone. They have a team that they can depend on when things get difficult. Here are a few things you can expect to come along with safety, belonging, and empowerment.[2345678910111213]

Safety fuels strength.

When people feel safe, they're not guarding themselves; they're growing. They speak up, take risks, and bounce back faster because they know they're not alone.

Empowered people don't quit; they commit.

Empowerment isn't about giving people control over everything. It's about giving them clarity, autonomy, and support. That's what builds commitment, not just compliance.

Belonging builds the bench.

When someone feels like they're truly part of the team, not just filling a role, they're more likely to stay, develop, and invest in others. It creates a culture of mutual care and accountability.

Resilience is a team sport.

We all hit hard moments. Belonging means no one carries the weight alone. Empowerment means people have the tools to recover and keep moving.

Retention is emotional before it's rational.

People don't leave jobs; they leave cultures where they feel invisible or stuck. When they feel seen, supported, and stretched, they stay.

📖 Storytime: The Cost of Belonging Without Voice

I once worked in a culture that hired incredible people who were smart, capable, and passionate. On paper, it was a dream team.

But once you were inside, the tone shifted.

Leaders micromanaged. Feedback wasn't asked for, and when it was offered, it often landed with a thud, or worse, was met with dismissive comments like, "Not everyone wants to know what you're thinking." That one stuck with me.

Most of the leaders I knew felt frustrated. Handcuffed. Undervalued.

They weren't trying to challenge authority; they were trying to contribute. But slowly, they stopped speaking up. Eventually, I was the only voice speaking out, the "troublemaker".

It's hard to own your work in a place where you don't feel like your voice belongs.

This wasn't just a culture issue; it was a belonging issue.

Because when people feel like their input doesn't matter, they stop taking initiative. They stop giving feedback. They start playing small.

Eventually, I realized something hard but honest: I didn't belong there anymore.

Not because I wasn't capable, but because the culture didn't have space for voices like mine.

So I left. And I learned something I'll never forget:

Lesson Learned: Belonging isn't just about being invited to the table. It's about being able to speak and be heard once you're there.

When was the last time your team felt heard, not just surveyed?

Personalized Accountability Is Not Favoritism; it's Exception Management

Exception Management is essential to leadership. Fair doesn't mean everyone gets the same; it means everyone gets what they need to be successful. Great leaders don't treat everyone identically; they treat everyone equitably.

Ask yourself:

- What motivates this person?

- What support do they need to grow?

- What clarity are they missing?

- What do they value most?

Fair doesn't mean *identical*. It means *intentional*. High-performing leaders adjust their *style*, not their *standards*.

⊘ *Example:*

One team member may be new and need more direction and structure, while another is consistently performing and thrives with more autonomy. You may meet more frequently with a newer hire but still expect the same results from both leaders.

When you know your team, their drivers, blockers, and communication styles, you can lead them with precision. And that precision creates trust.

Know How Each Person Is Wired to Build Trust

Know What You're Working With!

Everyone has a "user manual." To lead your team well, get curious about:

- Their communication preferences

- Their motivation style (recognition, autonomy, growth)

- How they receive feedback

- What shuts them down

Use a Meet & Greet or 1-on-1 starter form with prompts like:

- What do you love doing in your free time?

- What motivates you most at work?

- How do you like to receive praise?

- What's something a past manager did that helped you grow?

- What gives you energy at work?

- What are you great at?

- What does great leadership look like to you?

- What's one thing that would help you feel more supported?

- How do you prefer to receive feedback?

Another option is to build simple rituals to gather this data, such as onboarding forms, stay interviews, and team-building activities. The more you know, the more you can align accountability with how they're wired.

Build Trust and Honesty Will Follow

Accountability conversations require honesty, but honesty only happens when trust is present. If people feel judged, ignored, or unsafe, they won't tell you the truth. They'll tell you what they think you want to hear.

Trust is built in the small moments:

- Following through on your word

- Listening without fixing

- Admitting when you're wrong

- Coaching before correcting

You earn trust through consistency, curiosity, and care.

Coach Quen Says: "Culture is created when words and actions are in alignment".

If you say you value feedback but shut people down when it's inconvenient, trust erodes. If you reward results but ignore toxic behavior, safety disappears.

But when your behavior matches your message, people trust it. And when they trust it, they engage. *And when they engage, you get the best of them.*

 Leadership Challenge: Quick Trust Builder Exercise

Ask each team member:

- What makes you feel most supported as a teammate?

- What should I know about how you handle feedback?

- What's one way I can help you be at your best?

Leaders who ask these questions send a powerful signal: "I see you, and I care about more than performance."

Closing

Belonging and trust get you engagement, commitment, and retention. When you have trust among the individuals on your team, you can inspire, challenge, and motivate the group to accomplish more than they ever imagined. Remember, learning happens in reflection; let's reflect.[14]

Leadership Reflection:

- Who on my team might be lacking clarity, not commitment?

- What am I assuming people know about expectations, goals, or values?

- Where am I showing trust, and where might I be withholding it?

- What's one way I can connect more personally this week?

Coach Quen's Tip: You're not just managing results. You're shaping culture. When your team feels like they belong, they'll show up like they own it.

In the next chapter, we'll move from knowing your people to leading your role with clarity. Because accountability isn't just about others, it's also about how you show up, model standards, and own your role.

---

1. Hodges, A., & Park, B. (2013). Oppositional identities: Dissimilarities in how women and men experience parent versus professional roles. Journal of Personality and Social Psychology; J. Pers. Soc. Psychol., 105(2), 193-216.

2. Hodges, A., & Park, B. (2013). Oppositional identities: Dissimilarities in how women and men experience parent versus professional roles. Journal of Personality and Social Psychology; J. Pers. Soc. Psychol., 105(2), 193-216

3. Bem, S. L. (1981). Gender schema theory: A cognitive account of sex typing. Psychological Review, 88(4), 354-364.

4. Hoyt, C. L., & Simon, S. (2011). Female leaders: Injurious or inspiring role models for women? Psychology of Women Quarterly, 35(1), 143-157.

5. Berdahl, J. L., Cooper, M., Glick, P., Livingston, R. W., & Williams, J. C. (2018). Work as a masculinity contest. Journal of Social Issues, 74(3), 422-448.

6. Duchek, S., Raetze, S., & Scheuch, I. (2019). The role of diversity in organizational resilience. Business Research (Göttingen), 13(2), 387-423. doi:10.1007/s40685-019-0084-8

7. Zhou, H., & Chen, J. (2021). How does psychological empowerment prevent emotional exhaustion? Psychological safety and organizational embeddedness as mediators. *Frontiers in Psychology, 12*, 546687.

8. Singh, B., & Shaffer, M. A. (2018). Antecedents of organizational and community embeddedness: The roles of support, psychological safety, and need to belong. *Journal of Organizational Behavior, 39*(6), 758–772.

9. Hartley, M. (2024). Enhancing employee engagement and retention: The critical role of psychological safety in the onboarding process. *Strategic HR Review, 23*(1).

10. Saghar, H. (2024). *Talent management and its contribution to employee productivity: Investigating the interplay of psychological safety, person-organization fit, and employee performance in the telecom sector* [Master's thesis, National University of Sciences and Technology].

11. Lee, H. (2023). Organization resilience and organizational commitment: The roles of emotion appraisal and psychological safety. *Journal of Applied Psychology and Organizational Studies.*

12. Modise, J. M. (2023). The impacts of employee workplace empowerment, effective commitment and performance: An organizational systematic review. *International Journal of Human Resource Studies.*

13. Waseem, M., Khan, K., & Kiran, R. (2024). Fostering employee loyalty: The role of inclusive leadership in fostering organizational commitment through the mediating effect of psychological safety and perceived organizational support. *Journal of Facilities Management, 22(2).*

14. Schön, D. A. (1983). *The reflective practitioner: How professionals think in action.* Basic Books.

Chapter Five

Lead Your Role First: Model the Standard (Step 3)

The Most Overlooked Form of Accountability

You can't ask others to own their lane if you're drifting in yours.

Before you can hold others to the standard, you have to *lead your role with consistency, pride, and integrity*. Teams notice when:

- You miss deadlines

- You're unclear about your own expectations

- You react instead of lead

- Your actions are misaligned with your language

This is where credibility is won or lost.

📖 Storytime: Credibility and the Cost of the Quick Hire

I once hired a leader I knew could get results. I also knew, deep down, that his values didn't align with the organization. But I was under pressure. We needed someone. And I panicked.

I call it the "going to the grocery store hungry" mistake.

You know the one. You walk in starving and come out with snacks, chips, soda, none of the good stuff. No protein. No substance. Just quick energy. No nourishment. That's exactly what I did with this hire.

Yes, he drove results. But how he did it? That wasn't leadership.

He led through fear. He was all carrot or stick, no vision, no trust, no development.

And, at first, it looked like things were working. Until they weren't.

In less than a year:

- *We lost strong, values-driven leaders*

- *HR complaints were filed*

- *Morale took a nosedive*

- *And I, the one who made the hire, lost credibility with my team*

I had to let him go. But the damage had already been done. That experience taught me something I'll never forget: You don't just hire for results. You hire for how those results are achieved. Because in a culture of accountability, how and what are equally important. And as a leader, your credibility is your culture's foundation. Lose it, and you risk losing the very people you're trying to lead.

And when a senior leader called to ask me, "What happened with this one? It was costly". I just said, "I happened". I knew better; this was why I did it, and this is what I learned. All he could say was, "Well, ok". This was the first time in this entire situation I truly took accountability.

Hiring someone whose methods contradict your values, even if they get results, sends a louder message than any vision statement ever could.

Credibility is built when your words and your actions match. It's lost when the short-term win costs you long-term trust. When you lead your role first, you make decisions that don't just move the team forward; they move it in the right direction.

Lesson Learned: Leadership isn't just about what you do; it's about what you permit, what you prioritize, and what you reinforce.

Positional Pride Builds Cultural Credibility

Too many leaders slip into management mode, over-functioning for others instead of *owning their leadership lane.* I always say, stop doing other people's jobs and promote everyone to their own positions.[123]

When you are operating outside your core role, who is doing your job? When I worked in retail stores and walked in and saw a store manager on a register, I would immediately say, "Oh, who's doing your job?", which is leading the team and the business. When you vacate your position, there is a huge gap in leadership, direction, and alignment.[4]

Positional pride isn't arrogance; it's ownership of your leadership role and responsibilities.

What this looks like:

- You have a clear plan and priorities for your function or team

- You consistently communicate and reinforce values

- You respond to challenges without drama

- You embody the standards, not just enforce them

This is what gives your message *weight*.

The Rules of Ownership

Coach Quen's Rules of Ownership

- Own the Outcome – Don't just complete tasks; commit to results.

- Own the Message – Don't pass the buck; deliver clarity even when it's hard.

- Own the Moment – Don't deflect blame; own your impact and influence.

- Own the Model – Don't expect what you don't demonstrate.

- Own the details – Don't expect your teams to know the details if you don't.

In order to follow the rules of ownership, there are a few things you must do consistently as a leader before you can say you are leading your role with pride.

What the Best Leaders Do Consistently[567891011]

- Set Clear Expectations

- Communicate Effectively

- Exception Manage

- Build Relationships and Trust

- Narrow Focus and Priorities

- Monitor Progress and Provide Feedback

- Establish Clear Metrics and Milestones

- Address Barriers to Success

- Provide Necessary Resources

- Ensure Clarity of Message

- Lead by Example

If you are out of breath at the end of the list, you are not the only one. I have had people in workshops say, "Goodness" when we get to the end of the list.

Leadership is hard; if it wasn't, everyone would be a leader. The good news is with focus and intention, this list of behaviors becomes part of your consistent and dependable leadership routines.

⚖ **Leadership Challenge:**

Ask yourself: Where am I modeling the "Best Leaders Do Consistently" list well? Where am I off? Highlight the ones you are doing well and circle the ones you need to improve. Ask your boss and two direct reports to do the same for you.

Development and Feedback Escalation Map

If development and results aren't moving, you, as the leader, must do something different to develop your team. Don't just restate the expectation; get closer to the business. You won't know where to develop if you don't know what's broken. Finding the root cause of an issue is only possible if you know the details, get closer, and shadow the person and the process.

The development and feedback grid gives structure to how quickly you should move based on the impact or frequency of events.

⊘ *Example:*

There is a director who reports to you, and they consistently miss deadlines. Typically, they come and ask questions the day before the project is due. This means if they are not on track with the expectation, they will be asking for an extension. According to the development and feedback grid:

- The first time this happens, you can restate the expectations and ask what support they need from you.

- The second occurrence is when you, as a leader, must do something different. This is where you have options but you must do something.

  ◦ You escalate and get closer to the business.

- You shadow the leader on their team calls to look for clear direction being cascaded.

- You have direct conversations about the impact, consequences, and next steps.

- You include additional touch points to check for milestones in the project.

There are many things you can do as you travel down the map. The point is to do something different.

You can't continue to restate the expectation and think you will get a different outcome. It is your responsibility as the leader to develop and give feedback. You can't do that if your go-to-move is to restate and say, "Well, I told them".

DEVELOPMENT AND FEEDBACK MAP

Occurrence	Example Situation	Leadership Action
First	Team member misses a deadline	Clarify the expectation & reset support
Second	Pattern repeats	Have a direct conversation about impact & accountability. Get closer to the business and the leader.
Third	Still no shift	Escalate - align on consequence with performance improvement plans

Go to the Bonus Downloads chapter for access to a full Development and Feedback Map.

Most leaders either escalate too early (reactive) or too late (avoidant). This map helps leaders understand when to escalate and some actions that will help them move behaviors and the results.

Use this to normalize holding the line without drama or delay.

This map is important because it helps you and the team define and hold standards.

When You Let Go of Your Standards, You Confuse the Culture

Every time you excuse a miss, bend the standard, or justify the exception (without clarity), the team gets a new message. And it's louder than you think.

They don't hear, "I'm giving you grace." They hear:

- This doesn't really matter.

- We only mean it when things are going well.

- The standard shifts based on mood, pressure, or personality.

- The leader isn't serious.

Leadership isn't about being liked; it's about being trusted to mean what you say.

Once the team questions your consistency, they'll quietly begin to question your credibility.

Not all at once. Not out loud. But gradually:

- They'll delay deliverables.

- They'll do the minimum.

- They'll stop holding each other accountable because you've stopped modeling it yourself.

You may think you're being kind. Flexible. Empathetic. But without clarity, you're creating confusion. Without follow-through, you're creating inconsistency. And without consistency, there is a culture of chaos.

That doesn't mean you can't be human. You can absolutely offer grace. But grace still needs a boundary.

Leadership isn't about being liked. *It's about being trusted to mean what you say, even when it's uncomfortable, inconvenient, or unpopular.*

When your team knows the standard is real and that you live by it first, they rise to meet it. Not out of fear. But out of respect, clarity, and belief.

Closing

Trust and credibility are built over time but lost in a moment. You must lead your role first before you expect to be successful at leading others. Whether you abdicate your responsibilities or own your role with clarity and conviction, your team will follow your lead.

⛰ Leadership Challenge:

Ask: Where have I bent the bar lately, and what message might that be sending? Make a list of each occurrence over the last 90 days. Ensure you include the message you might be sending.

Check Your Ownership Blind Spots

�※ Leadership Reflection:

- What part of my role have I been neglecting, avoiding, or reacting to?

- Where have I softened the standard I claim to uphold?

- Where do I need to reset my own discipline before expecting it from others?

📢

Coach Quen Says: "Leadership is meeting the team where they are and helping them get to where they, the business, and the team need and want to be".

---

1. **Kanayeva, G. (2019).** *Facilitating teacher leadership in Kazakhstan* [Doctoral dissertation, University of Cambridge].

2. **Kramer, C. A. (2014).** *Changes in military leaders' transformational leadership styles after trauma* [Doctoral dissertation, Capella University].

3. **McDevitt, P., & Fitzpatrick, M. (2020).** *Anchoring cultural change and organizational change: Case study research evaluation project All Hallows College Dublin 1995-2015.* Cambridge Scholars Publishing.

4. **Bayer, C. F. (2012).** *The impact of supervision, evaluation, and systemic issues on the efficacy of the role of the school counselor* [Doctoral dissertation, Immaculata University].

5. Van Den Akker, L., Heres, L., & Lasthuizen, K. M. (2009). Ethical leadership and trust: It's all about meeting expectations. Vrije Universiteit Amsterdam.

6. Yukl, G. (2012). Effective leadership behavior: What we know and what questions need more attention. Academy of Management Perspectives, 26(4), 66–85.

7. Wong, C. A., & Cummings, G. G. (2009). The influence of authentic leadership behaviors on trust and work outcomes of health care staff. Journal of Leadership Studies, 3(2), 6–23.

8. Hasel, M. C., & Grover, S. L. (2017). An integrative model of trust and leadership. Leadership & Organization Development Journal, 38(6), 849–867.

9. Podsakoff, P. M., MacKenzie, S. B., & Moorman, R. H. (1990). Transformational leader behaviors and their effects on followers' trust in leader, satisfaction, and organizational citizenship behaviors. The Leadership Quarterly, 1(2), 107–142.

10. Strang, K. D. (2007). Examining effective technology project leadership traits and behaviors. Computers in Human Behavior, 23(2), 424–462.

11. Behrendt, P., Matz, S., & Göritz, A. S. (2017). An integrative model of leadership behavior. The Leadership Quarterly, 28(1), 229–244.

Chapter Six

Align: Make Expectations Crystal Clear (Step 4)

Clarity Is the Cornerstone of Accountability

People can't own what they don't understand.

When expectations are vague:

- People underperform without realizing it

- Teams duplicate effort or drop the ball

- Leaders micromanage or over-explain

- Frustration replaces feedback

Clarity is a form of kindness. Alignment is a form of respect. As Dr. Brene Brown says, "Clear is Kind. Unclear is Unkind".[1]

The Anatomy of a Clear Expectation

Use this five-part Clarity Framework to define expectations with precision:[23456789]

Element	Description	Example
WHAT	The task or deliverable	"Complete the client report"
HOW	The standard or method	"Using the new reporting format and peer feedback"
WHY	The business context or value	"So the leadership team can prep for the board meeting"
WHO	The role or person responsible	"You, as the account lead"
WHEN	The deadline or cadence	"By Friday at 2pm"

Coach Quen's Tip: Every task or objective should be reviewed through this Clarity Framework lens.

Common Signs of Misalignment

Misalignment happens. The key is to catch it quickly and correct it.[1011]

Even experienced teams fall into these traps:

- Misinterpreting priorities ("I thought this was low urgency")

- Assuming roles ("I didn't know it was my job")

- Working from outdated instructions ("That's how we used to do it...")

- Doing good work, but not the right work ("I thought this was the priority")

When these happen repeatedly, it's not a motivation problem; it's a clarity problem.

If your team doesn't have clarity of priorities, direction, and vision, they have been set up for failure. There is no other way to say it.

I once worked with a woman whose team gave feedback that they wanted more direction and a narrow focus. She told me, "They can read it in the shared folder". That response, while easy for her, leaves the team set up for failure. Clarity is one of the most important things you can and must do for your team.

Tools for Alignment

Below, I have listed a few tools I use in coaching and workshops:

Core Roles

Start With: An in-depth job description (JD).

Define: The 3–5 most essential functions for each role.

Ask: If this role disappeared, what would break? That's your core.

Note: While there are other things in the JD and a list of necessary functions, the core role should be narrow, essential to the success of the organization, and reviewed with the team quarterly for alignment.

IDPs (Individual Development Plans)

Start With: Organizational leadership competencies, recent feedback, and consistent feedback.

Define: The two strengths and two development areas for each person. Each team member should own this process for themselves and then align with their leader.

Ask: How have I accomplished my biggest achievements, and what feedback have I received that I need to improve?

Note: Select on the job actions that develop the individual in the areas identified. Make expectations visible through development conversations. Link growth to impact.

Rules of Engagement - Lead the team to clarify how they:

- Engages and communicates

- Gives feedback

- Makes decisions

- Handles missed expectations

- Shares accountability

📖 Storytime: The Rules We Write. The Culture We Build

I had a leader on my team who was deeply proud of her business and of her people. She was new to me as a direct report, but she was also new to the broader leadership team.

Because of that, I knew I needed to be intentional about building trust, not just between her and me but across the team as a whole.

We were headed into a team strategy session focused on succession planning, discussing district and store leaders, identifying gaps, and surfacing future talent.

Now, here's what I've learned: When you start talking about people's people, things can get heated, fast. So before we jumped into any succession conversations, I kicked off the day with a Rules of Engagement team builder.

Each person shared what they needed to feel safe and productive in the room. Together, we crafted a short list of how we'd show up for each other:

- *How we'd listen*

- *How we'd offer feedback*

- *How we'd handle disagreement*

- *How we'd protect the space*

- *Ultimately, how we would respect each other*

We agreed. We wrote it down. We posted it. And then... we started the talent conversation.

About three hours in, things got tense.

This leader became visibly defensive as feedback came in about one of her team members.

She started pushing back, hard. Voices elevated. Energy shifted. You could feel the room tighten.

And then something beautiful happened.

One of her peers, calm but clear, reached over, picked up the paper with our Rules of Engagement and held it up in the air. Didn't say a word. Just held it up.

We all paused.

And then we laughed, not in mockery, but in mutual relief. I called a break. The room exhaled.

That moment reminded me: Accountability doesn't just come from the boss. It comes from the team. That day, a piece of paper and a well-timed gesture did more than I could have as the leader in the room. Because the standard wasn't mine, it was ours.

Lesson Learned: Culture isn't protected by a title. It's protected by shared agreement, shared responsibility, and shared courage.

Leadership Challenge:

Does your team know the rules of engagement, or are they assuming them?

Have each team member make a list of what's most important to them in teamwork. If they are similar, document it and post it. If they are not, conduct a Rules of Engagement exercise to align the team. Or you can jump straight to the engagement exercise. There's something unifying about people discussing their expectations. While they may use different words, it really comes down to the fact that we all want to be respected.

Clarity and Candor Are Caring

"Unspoken expectations are premeditated resentments".[12] Dr. Brené Brown

Lack of clarity isn't neutral; it creates:

- Confusion

- Second-guessing

- Resentment

- Delay

Use *Clarity and Candor* are Caring as a mantra:

- In direction

- In roles

- In delegation

- In coaching

- In feedback given and received

Accountability Check-In Questions

Ask:

- What does success look like in this role/project?

- What do I assume they understand but haven't actually said?

- Where are roles overlapping, creating friction?

One thing I learned on my leadership journey is to ask the question:

Who owns this, and who supports it?

As one of my favorite bosses used to say, who has the full handprint of ownership? Many people have fingerprints on things. Who is the owner? I have never forgotten that clear ownership message.

Remember a common leadership principle. "If it's everyone's job, it's no one's job."

Understand Core Roles and Who Owns What

If you have been humming and flipping through the rest of the book, please take note of this section. It's a game-changer!

When expectations aren't updated or documented:

- High performers get overloaded

- Others disengage

- People look for clarity in other leaders, not you

- Friction arises during cross-team work

- People work on what they think is most important

 Leadership Challenge: Run a role clarity activity quarterly:

- Everyone writes what they think they own and the priorities for the team to be successful.

- Compare, clarify, realign

- Reflect on how *you did*, not them

If there is confusion, you have to reflect on your ability to narrow the focus, communicate priorities, and clarify roles. Remember, from "the best leaders do all this stuff" list, you have a lot to do before you look at the team! Role clarity is where most accountability breakdowns begin and where most can be prevented.

Set Standards, Not Just Goals

Both the "how" and the "what" matter! A leader can accomplish goals the wrong way. They can drive a result through micromanagement, shortcuts, and a lack of root-cause problem-solving.

When leaders focus only on the what, they drive the concept that the only thing that matters is the result. When a leader focuses on the how and the what, they reinforce the culture of the organization and the values that guide behaviors.

By underscoring the how and the what, leaders drive their teams to accomplish long-term results aligned with strategy and values, not short-term results that don't serve the team or the organization for the long haul.

Goals tell you what to achieve.
Standards set the expectation of how you operate while achieving it.

Clear standards and values define:

- How work gets done (pace, tone, format, approach)

- How people behave when things go wrong

- What is rewarded, coached, or corrected

Standards and values give the team a path to long-term success.

Closing

Being specific removes ambiguity from a situation. When teams know what is expected of them, they are more confident in taking action and more likely to move forward to accomplish the task. Clarity is one of the greatest gifts you can give to your team.

☼ Leadership Reflection:

- What expectations have I implied but not stated?

- Where am I being clear in my own mind but not in my communication?

- What does my team believe "great" looks like, and is that aligned with me? Am I aligned with the organization?

In the next chapter, we'll explore how to lock in clarity with routines, the rhythms that make accountability sustainable, not situational.

---

1. Brown, Brené. *Dare to Lead: Brave Work. Tough Conversations. Whole Hearts.* Random House, 2018. (Referenced in workshops and interviews.)

2. Allert, J. R., & Chatterjee, S. R. (1997). Corporate communication and trust in leadership. *Journal of Communication Management, 2*(4), 356–367.

3. Charteris-Black, J. (2006). *The communication of leadership: The design of leadership style.* Routledge.

4. Featherstone, M. V. (2013). *The importance of clarity in educational leadership program goals* [Master's thesis, Boise State University]. Boise State ScholarWorks.

5. Gordon, G. (2002). The roles of leadership and ownership in building an effective quality culture. *Quality in Higher Education, 8*(1), 97–106.

6. Harrison, E. B., & Mühlberg, J. (2014). *Leadership communication: How leaders communicate and how communicators lead in today's global enterprise.* Business Expert Press.

7. Johansson, C. (2018). *Leadership communication.* ResearchGate.

8. Locke, E. A. (1999). *The essence of leadership: The four keys to leading successfully.* Lexington Books.

9. Moss, S. A., Butar Butar, I., Hirst, G., & Tice, M. (2014). *Leadership and strategy: The vital but evasive role of cooperation and clarity of expectations during strategic change.* Academia.

10. de Vries, J. A. (2015). Champions of gender equality: Female and male executives as leaders of gender change. Equality, Diversity and Inclusion: An International Journal, 34(1), 21-36.

11. Molefi, N., O'Mara, J., & Richter, A. (2021, April). Global diversity, equity and inclusion benchmark. The Center for Global Inclusion.

12. Brown, Brené. *Dare to Lead: Brave Work. Tough Conversations. Whole Hearts.* Random House, 2018. (Referenced in workshops and interviews.)

Chapter Seven

Routines: Drive Follow-Up & Follow-Through (Step 5)

Why Routines Matter More Than Reminders

You don't rise to the level of your intentions; you fall to the level of your systems.[1] James Clear said *goals* instead of *intentions,* but both fit nicely. The point is you must have great routines to live up to your goals and intentions.

Accountability isn't sustained by reminders, micromanagement, or last-minute fire drills.

It's sustained through routines, structure, and habits.

- Structure isn't about control; it's about *consistency, clarity, and care.*

- Routines are where your values become visible.

This is where accountability becomes real, not just something we say but something we practice.

What Great Leaders Build In: The Power of Routines

Let's be clear: high-performing teams don't "wing it." They move with a plan, not just speed.

These *routines give people the time, space, and safety to reflect, reset, and recommit.*

Core accountability routines include:[2345678]

- 1-on-1s with purpose

- Weekly team syncs with scorecard check-ins

- Monthly and quarterly business reviews

- Developmental plans (IDPs, skill plans)

- Feedback cadences (informal + formal)

These are not "extras". They are *essential leadership practices.*

Again, your team will not live up to their potential if you don't have structure, routines, follow-up, and a feedback loop. They just can't. Each will be moving at their own pace, in their own direction, focused on their own thing. This is not team success.

The Feedback Loop Is the Lifeline

In the absence of feedback:

- Assumptions grow

- Mistrust creeps in

- Accountability fades

Everyone needs feedback, but it's not fun. "Feedback is a Gift" is a common leadership saying, but I'm not crazy enough to think people receive it as a gift.

However, if you build feedback routines that make it part of an accountability culture, it will become part of how your team operates.

Routines help prevent silence and avoidance. When feedback is baked into the week and not saved for *when there's a problem*, it builds trust and keeps people engaged.

Coach Quen's Tip: If you're only giving feedback when something's off, you're reinforcing a reactive culture.

Storytime: Feedback, Comparison, and Becoming Part of the Solution

I worked in a corporate office for nearly ten years before moving into a field leadership role. My first real experience with an accountability culture? Let's just say it wasn't great.

And not because of the leader.
Because I didn't yet understand my part in the culture.

My boss would give me feedback, and I'd get defensive. I'd argue, explain, compare. I spent more time justifying my choices than listening to what could help me grow.

There was a peer on my team who always seemed to take feedback so well. She'd nod, ask clarifying questions, apply it, and keep moving. Meanwhile,

I was getting stuck. Frustrated. Even resentful. I started comparing myself to her so much that, if I'm being honest, I began to dislike her, and she hadn't done anything wrong.

One day, my boss finally sat me down and asked, "What are your goals?"

We had an honest conversation, not just about performance, but about where I wanted to go and what might be getting in the way. He helped me see that my habit of comparison was crowding out my capacity for growth.

It didn't shift overnight. But over time, I reflected more deeply.

And I realized something important: I trusted him.

I believed he had my best interest at heart. And more than that, I realized I was in control of how I responded, how I grew, and what I achieved.

So, I started listening, really listening. I applied the feedback. I worked on my mindset. I focused on my role. And little by little, my results moved. I got promoted to a senior analyst position. Then, only months later, I got another promotion to a new department as a first-time manager.

To this day, I credit that leader with teaching me one of the most valuable lessons of my career:

Accountability isn't just about being held to expectations. It's about owning your response, your growth, and your results.

He modeled what I now teach: that accountability lives where there's clarity of ownership, belief in purpose, and support along the way.

He gave me more than feedback. It was a master class in leadership and in growing up professionally.

Lesson Learned: Feedback is accepted when trust is present. With trust, intention can be believed, not questioned. When people know their leader has their best interest in mind, the feedback may hurt, but they will more likely take action to correct it.

Leadership Reflection:

Where am I resisting feedback when I could be receiving growth?
Is there anyone on my team resisting feedback? What can I do differently to help them through it?

1-on-1s: The Most Underutilized Leadership Tool

If you're not using 1-on-1s to coach for clarity, you're missing your most powerful lever.

High-impact 1-on-1s include:

- A check-in on progress and energy

- A pulse on what's unclear or blocked

- A space to reconnect to goals, results, and growth

Suggested timing:

- Weekly or bi-weekly 30-minute check-ins

- Use a simple structure: Wins, Challenges, Focus (aligned with priorities), Needs, and Due Date

Coach Quen's Tip: Send two reflection questions ahead of time to support the meeting with purpose.

Team Routines That Anchor Accountability

Team routines reinforce shared ownership and visibility.

To drive team collaboration, teamwork, and accountability, you should maximize the time the team spends together. Many people hate meetings because most are not productive. By having an intentional agenda, ownership for topics, and follow-up actions, you drive accountability in the meetings, not just meeting to meet.

⊘ **Examples:**

- *Weekly scorecard reviews: What's on track? What's at risk?*

- *Monthly "ownership roundups": Each team member shares one commitment they're proud of and one thing they're improving.*

- *Quarterly pulse checks or business reviews: What's working? What's unclear? What needs attention?*

Coach Quen's Tip: Remember you are always building trust. Have the first 3-5 minutes of each team call cover fun connection topics and recognition.

These rituals create space for alignment before things break down. Anchor the team with dependable routines, and trust will build.

Route vs. Routine: A Culture-Building Analogy

As I often say to clients, *"Your route gets you to a destination. Your routine shapes who you become on the way"*. This is what separates tactical leaders from transformational ones.

Many leaders focus only on routes (goals, milestones) but forget that routines are what build ownership.

- Want a culture of feedback? Build feedback into the routine.

- Want people to own their work? Normalize accountability check-ins.

- Want growth? Make development plans a standing item, not a once-a-year form.

Culture is built in the *repeatable*, not the remarkable.

SAMPLE ACCOUNTABILITY ROUTINE MAP

Routine	Cadence	Focus
1-on-1s	Weekly/Bi-weekly	Clarity, support, coaching, feedback, individual follow-up
Team Sync	Weekly	Progress, alignment, blockers, collaboration
Scorecard Review	Monthly	Metrics, trends, insights, course correction
Development Plans	Quarterly	Growth, career, strengths, opportunities, progress
Feedback Pulse	Ongoing	Trust, improvement, alignment

Your Leadership Opportunity

If you've ever said, "We already talked about this" or "Well, I told them", chances are, it's not a clarity issue. *It's a consistency issue.*

I've never met a leader who said, "Wow, I have so much free time today, I'm not sure what I'm going to do with it". If this is you, don't tell anyone, you won't win any friends.

Because our days are packed, we have to be more intentional in our communication. I often remind my clients that communication itself is not a success. For communication to be successful, the audience needs to hear, comprehend, respond, or act in accordance.

To increase your consistency of message and, as a result, the success of your communication, there are a few things you must do.

This is your moment to decide:

- What needs to be built into your leadership routine?

- What's been ad hoc that now needs to be intentional?

- Where is your team waiting for more structure, not more pressure?

Closing

I will repeat how I opened the chapter. Structure isn't about control; it's about consistency, clarity, and care. Over-orchestrating can be frustrating to teams, but no structure at all will set the stage for failure. Care enough about the group to give structure and consistency. They will reward you with trust and engagement.

✲ **Leadership Reflection:**

- What routine is missing in my team's culture right now?

- What meeting do I need to upgrade instead of cancel?

- What meeting do I need to cancel or reduce the number of participants?

- Where could a 10-minute check-in prevent a 10-week issue?

Now that we've built the five essential steps, it's time to shift from insight to integration. In the next chapter, we'll help you move from agreement to action and build a real plan for culture change that sticks.

---

1. Clear, J. (2018). *Atomic habits: An easy & proven way to build good habits & break bad ones*. Avery.

2. Gostick, A., & Elton, C. (2018). *The best team wins: The new science of high performance*. Simon and Schuster.

3. Ahmad, N. R. (2025). Exploring the relationship between leadership styles and employee motivation in remote work environments. *Al-Aasar Journal of Research and Development, 1*(1).

4. Mattson, H., Zoffel, J., & McCormick, M. (2023). Systems reviews: An approach to building coherence, increasing efficiency, and improving workflow at state education agencies. *ERIC Institute of Education Sciences.*

5. Neves, R. (2024). *The engineering leadership playbook: Strategies for team success and business growth.* Springer.

6. Neves, R. (2024). Collaboration and team dynamics. In *The engineering leadership playbook* (Chapter 3). Springer.

7. Rogelberg, S. G. (2024). *Glad we met: The art and science of 1:1 meetings.* Oxford University Press.

8. Wisdom, J. (2023). *Five ways to make your one-on-one meetings more effective.* ReportDS.

PART III

INTEGRATION & ACTION

Chapter Eight

From Agreement to Action: Making It Real

It's about building a plan, committing to it, and closing the gap between what we say we value and how we lead daily.

Insight alone doesn't change culture. Implementation does. You've done the hard work, self-awareness, team alignment, clarifying expectations, and building routines.

Now comes the real work: *putting it all into motion.*

Accountability isn't built in theory; it's built in the decisions you make and the behaviors you repeat.

Many leaders agree with the idea of accountability...but still don't act. Why?

Because acting requires:

- Vulnerability

- Consistency

- Saying no to old patterns

- Leading in a new way, before it's comfortable

As a Co-Active trained coach, I believe that the "being and do-ing" have to be present for sustainable change. According to the Co-Active Training Institute, *being* is why the action and behavior change is important to you. Doing is the action you must take for forward movement and change. Both are vital, and transformation only occurs when each is present.[1]

The Culture Development Plan

It's time to build a real plan. Not just a list of hopes but a real path forward.

Think of this as your team's *Accountability Culture Reset.*

Break this into three areas:

Modeling

- Ask:

  - What am I modeling now?

  - What message is my team receiving from how I show up?

  - What's one standard I need to return to or recommit to?

Self-check: Do my actions match my values?

Messaging

- Ask:

  - Where am I being vague?

  - What expectations have I assumed are clear but never said?

- What systems or rituals do I need to reintroduce?

- What communication style does each individual need to be successful?

Coach Quen's Tip: Use the 5-part Clarity Framework in Chapter 6 to help.

Momentum

- Ask:

    - What feedback am I avoiding?

    - What needs follow-up?

    - What's one conversation I need to have this week to build trust?

    - What routines do I need to get more intentional about?

Make It Real: The 30-Day Culture Sprint

Culture doesn't shift during a retreat. It shifts through consistent routines.

Design a 30-day sprint with intentional focus:

Week	Focus	Action
Week 1	Model the Standard	• Reintroduce key expectations and align with the team's expectations. • Lead a values huddle. • Connect the why to the organizational vision and values. • Identify and share as a team strengths, opportunities, triggers, and overuse for yourself and each person on the team.
Week 2	Clarify the Message	• Run a Role Clarity or Expectations Reset session. • Identify ownership and support roles in key priorities. • Ask the team where clarity is lacking.
Week 3	Build Routines	• Launch a weekly team check-in or scorecard sync. • Create detailed agendas with priorities, feedback, and follow-up sections. • Schedule IDP quarterly sessions for the year.
Week 4	Reinforce & Reflect	• Ask for feedback and build quarterly feedback routines. • Reflect on what shifts as you make changes. Capture the learning. • Step back and shadow to check progress.

Closing

You may be great at everything discussed in this book, or you may have gaps the size of the Grand Canyon. Wherever you are, there is no shame. *The only shame would be if you have the information you need to build the culture you desire and don't act.*

From agreement to action, hopefully, you make a plan to keep reflecting and growing.

1. Kimsey-House, H., Kimsey-House, K., Sandahl, P., & Whitworth, L. (2018). Co-active coaching: The proven framework for transformative conversations at work and in life (4th ed.). Nicholas Brealey Publishing.

Chapter Nine

Accountability Conversations That Work

Using the 5 Cs to Create Clarity, Courage, and Culture

Why Most Accountability Conversations Don't Work

Most conversations about accountability come too late after a pattern has formed, results have slipped, or resentment has built. Leaders often delay the conversation because they fear:

- Making the situation worse

- Damaging the relationship

- Being seen as "too harsh"

But when leaders delay, the result is worse. As Colin Powell said, "Bad news isn't wine.[1] It doesn't improve with age". Delay creates:

- Mistrust grows

- Expectations erode

- Team performance suffers

Accountability conversations don't create conflict. They reveal conflict. And, when done well, they resolve it.

Introducing Coach Quen's 5 Cs of Courageous Conversations

This framework gives leaders a repeatable model for holding people accountable without damaging the relationship.

The 5 C's	Definition
Clarity	Be clear about what needs to be said and why it matters. No ambiguity.
Candor	Be honest and direct. Don't sugarcoat, but don't bulldoze either.
Curiosity	Ask before assuming. Stay open to learning, not just correcting.
Credibility	Your message lands better when it comes from someone who walks the talk.
Consistency	Make courageous conversations a habit, not a surprise.

When leaders master these five elements, accountability discussions become a conversation, not a confrontation.

Anatomy of a Courageous Conversation

Here's a script-style breakdown to walk through the five Cs in real time:

Step 1 – Clarity
I want to check in on something I've noticed. We agreed the report

would be sent by Thursday, and it came on Friday afternoon. That's not what we aligned on.

Step 2 – Candor
This isn't about catching a mistake; It's about staying consistent with what we've said matters.

Step 3 – Curiosity
Can you help me understand what happened from your side?

Step 4 – Credibility
I know we've had a few weeks of shifting deadlines, and I own that. But it's important that we rebuild trust around timelines.

Step 5 – Consistency
Let's get back to our agreed expectations and talk about what support or clarity you need to hit them consistently.

Accountability Is Not One Conversation, It's a Culture

One tough conversation won't fix an unclear or inconsistent culture. Routines and consistency are essential to the culture.

Accountability conversations must be:

- *Ongoing,* not one-time

- *Developmental,* not disciplinary

- *Two-way,* not top-down

When done well, they:

- Build resilience

- Deepen trust

- Create clarity before resentment builds

Coach Quen's Tip: Ask team members to give you feedback, too. Normalize mutual accountability.

Conversation Cues for Common Scenarios

Here are a few common situations and a script that walk you through possible discussion prompts.

Missed Deadline (again) - "I noticed we've had a few missed deadlines on this project. Let's talk through what's going on and how we can reset expectations together."

Pattern of Defensiveness - "I want to check in. I've noticed it's been hard to give feedback lately, and that's not who we've been as a team. How are you experiencing these conversations?"

Misalignment on Role or Results - "I think we might have different views of what success looks like in this role. Can we revisit our expectations and make sure we're on the same page?"

When You Feel the Tension, Name the Tension

If energy shifts, don't ignore it, address it:

- "I'm sensing some frustration, and I want to make sure we're aligned, not just compliant."

- "This is uncomfortable, but that's okay. It means we care. Let's stay in it."

- "I know this conversation isn't fun. Let's take a 10-minute break so we can both refresh and collect our thoughts. I want to make sure we uphold our normal interaction pattern which is very respectful."

- "Our conversation is getting a little off track. Let's review our Rules of Engagement and resume the conversation when we are aligned again."

Accountability requires emotional intelligence. Leaders who acknowledge tension without escalating it create space for truth. Leaders who don't shift with the situation create anxiety and fracture the trust they have worked hard to build.

Courage Before Comfort

You won't always feel "ready." That's okay.

Courageous conversations don't get easier. You just become better at having them. The minute you are excited to have a tough conversation void of dignity and respect is the minute you should hang up your leadership hat.

Coach Quen's Tip: You can always approach conversations with dignity and respect.

Use this simple mantra: "Clarity now avoids confusion later".

And remember: the tone you bring to the conversation is just as important as the words you choose.

Accountability Conversation Checklist

Before you initiate a conversation, ask yourself:

- Have I been clear in the past about what was expected?

- Am I leading with care, not just correction?

- Have I created psychological safety in this relationship?

- Am I willing to listen, not just speak?

- Am I willing to follow up consistently?

- Have I selected the right time and place to have the conversation?

Close with Confidence and Care

"I'm naming this because I believe in your potential and want to support your success. Let's reset and move forward together. We will circle back during our one-on-one next week to see how things are going and what support you need."

Following the 5 Cs framework will help your conversation be intentional and leave space for mutual dialogue.

If You've Done It All, You've Done It All

There are times in leadership when, despite your best efforts, nothing changes.

You've been self-aware.

You've invested in the relationship.

You've owned your role.

You've communicated clearly and specifically.

You've put strong routines in place to support follow-through.

And still... nothing moves.

Sometimes, *it's simply not the right fit.*

And while that's hard, it's also okay.

What's not okay is allowing someone to stay stuck and making the rest of the team miserable in the process because you're avoiding a hard decision.

Here's the truth: most people know when they're not doing well.

They wake up with a pit in their stomach every day.

They dread Monday.

They feel the tension. So does the team.

That's no way to lead. And it's no way to live.

Sometimes, the kindest thing you can do is help someone move on, not out of punishment but out of purpose.

And if you "go to the grocery store hungry" and make the same mistake I did, you must move fast. When you hire from urgency instead of alignment, the cost shows up later.

If you realize you brought in the wrong person, not because they're bad, but because they're not right for the role, the culture, or the team, don't delay. Move fast. Don't hesitate.

The longer you wait, the more it costs:

- The team's morale

- The culture's clarity

- Your own credibility

Correcting the mistake quickly isn't failure; it's leadership.

You're not just managing one person. You're protecting the integrity of the entire team.

Remember:

Kindness is clarity.
Leadership is alignment.
Accountability means helping others see when it's time to shift or step forward into something that better fits their strengths, their energy, and their season.

You're not just leading for today.
You're protecting the health of the whole culture.
And sometimes, that means letting go with compassion but also with conviction.

Closing

Yes, challenging conversations can be difficult. Yes, you want to preserve people's feelings and dignity. Yes, you want everyone to feel like a superstar. The only way to accomplish all of this is to move through the tough parts and get to the parts that help people increase their efficacy, grow to their potential, and achieve their goals. By withholding information that can open this door for individuals, you are truly impacting futures, not in a good way. While it can be tough, I know you can do it!

Leadership Reflection:

- Who have I been avoiding a conversation with?

- What pattern have I been tolerating instead of addressing?

- Which of the 5 Cs do I need to strengthen most in my leadership?

- When will I schedule and prepare for one accountability conversation this week?

5 Cs Accountability Conversation Planner - Check out the Bonus Downloads for a document to help you plan challenging conversations.

In the final chapter, we'll talk about sustaining the culture of accountability you've worked so hard to build through feedback loops, recognition, and continuous recalibration.

---

1. *It Worked for Me: In Life and Leadership* by Colin Powell, Harper, 2012.

Chapter Ten

Sustaining the Culture: Feedback, Adaptation & Wins

Culture Doesn't Stick Without Sustaining It

Accountability isn't a checklist. It's a commitment. And even the most intentional culture needs ongoing attention.

Culture isn't what you launch. It's what you grow and protect.

Without consistent reinforcement:

- New habits fade

- Communication breaks down

- People revert to old norms

Leaders must act quickly to call out old norms or new habits fade, fast. Reinforcement must happen consistently, not as an event.

Build Feedback Loops That Keep You Connected

High-performing leaders build closed loops, not loose ends.

Ways to keep the pulse:

- Quarterly pulse checks: Ask what's working, what's unclear, and what's off-track

- 360 feedback moments: Not just performance reviews, but peer and upward insights

- Team post reflection: Reflect together after major projects or milestones

- Feedback in Action: Normalize informal check-ins, voice notes, quick syncs

Coach Quen's Tip: If you're not gathering feedback, you're guessing, and you're likely wrong.

Recognize Accountability in Action and Celebrate Culture Wins

People need to see that accountability is valued, not just expected.

If you find you are only giving feedback when things go wrong, recalibrate and ensure you are giving positive feedback on exact behaviors and results.

People tend to repeat the behaviors that are seen, appreciated, and acknowledged. If there are behaviors that are making the individual or team successful, call that out. Don't miss the opportunity to reinforce great behaviors.

Don't just celebrate metrics; celebrate how the team achieved them.

Celebrate: The What and the How

- Follow-through under pressure

- Proactive ownership of issues

- Courageous conversations

- Values-driven decisions

Say Things Like:

- This win happened because of ownership.

- This recovery showed our feedback culture in motion.

- That handoff reflected everything we said we value.

Recognition builds momentum:

- Call it out in team meetings

- Share quick stories of "Accountability in Action

- Create a peer-nomination process for team shoutouts

What gets celebrated gets repeated. Culture comes to life in the wins you name and the behaviors you reinforce.

Normalize Course-Correction Without Shame

Every team drifts. Every plan hits bumps. The difference is *how leaders respond.*

The best leaders don't wait for perfection; they coach for progress.

What to do when things go sideways:

- Reground in expectations, values, and purpose

- Lead a reset conversation: "Here's what we said, here's what's happening, let's recalibrate"

- Invite your team into the solution: "What do we need to shift to realign?"

Coach Quen's Tip: Say to your team, "Let's learn forward, not punish backward".

While you need to address past behavior to correct future behavior, it should be from a learning perspective, not a punishing one.

Protect the Standard Without Becoming Rigid

As a leader who loves structure, even I have to admit that being too rigid can stifle creativity, innovation, and critical thinking. High-accountability cultures are not harsh; they're clear and human. Leaving room for people.

Sustaining the culture means:

- Keeping the standard high

- Offering support when people slip

- Leading with grace and grit

- Being curious when things go wrong

Accountability is firm, not forceful. It holds space for both excellence and empathy.

Watch for Drift and Recommit Publicly

We all have a lot going on in a day: unexpected meetings, traffic, family emergencies, due dates, etc.

Even the best leaders have challenges keeping up, fall out of great routines, and have to course correct.

Most times, it's easier to let something go, "just this once". Remember, small cracks are what eventually break the culture of accountability. So, reflect, rejuvenate, and recommit when it happens to you.

Even the strongest leaders slip into:

- Over-functioning

- Vague direction

- Letting things slide

Build in moments to *publicly recommit* to the culture:

- During one-on-ones: "Remind me where you are in this project, and let's align on due dates."

- At quarterly meetings: "Here's what we are recommitting to as a team."

- After key milestones: "Let's realign and check ourselves."

Use these checkpoints to reflect:

- What's shifted?

- What's slipping?

- What do we need to reinforce?

Make Accountability Visible, Not Just Vocal

As we have aligned, routines are essential to building an excellent accountability culture. Make a note in your journal now. How will you build accountability into routines?

Embed accountability routines in:

- Onboarding rituals

- Meeting cadences

- Performance reviews

- Recognition systems

- Development sessions

Use tools like:

- Business Reviews to track clarity, consistency, and follow-through

- Team meetings, check-ins, and one-on-ones (teamwide) to reflect engagement and ownership

- Leader self-audits to align behavior with values. Ask: "What do I need to do differently, or where have I slipped?"

What isn't visible or measurable won't be sustainable.

Closing - Leadership Reflection & Renewal

Leadership Reflection:

- What behaviors am I seeing that reflect our culture?

- What have I let slip that I need to return to?

- Where is my team winning, and do they know it?

- What's one ritual I'll reinforce to keep the culture alive?

Accountability is not an event. It's a culture. And culture is leadership, day by day, conversation by conversation, choice by choice.

You now have the framework, tools, and language to build something powerful, not just a performing team, but a team that trusts, owns, and delivers together.

You don't need more fire drills. You need more follow-through, and now you have the plan to lead it and the culture to sustain it.

Go to the next chapter for bonus content and tools called out in the book. Get organized and get going. The sooner you start, the sooner you, your team, and your organization will benefit from a culture of accountability. ▨

BONUS
DOWNLOADS

Chapter Eleven

Bonus Downloads

Download your free tools by scanning the QR code below or clicking the link in your ebook.

https://shop.coachquen.com/products/the-accountability-advantage-digital-downloads

These tools are designed to help you turn insight into action. Use them during internal workshops, coaching sessions, or on your own time to deepen reflection and leadership impact. Brief instructions on how to use each tool are located on the net pages.

Values Worksheet

Use this exercise to clarify what drives you and how aligned your behavior is with what matters most.

Instructions:

1. Print or open the editable PDF.

2. Set a timer for 3 minutes and select your top 10 values, the words that resonate most.

3. Set a timer for 2 more minutes to narrow those 10 down to 5 values, then eliminate 2 more to land on your top 3 values.

4. Write down and define your top 3 leadership values. What do they mean to you personally?

5. On page 2, reflect on how well you're living those values:

   ○ Where are you aligned?

   ○ Where might you be overusing a strength?

   ○ Where are you out of sync?

Individual Development Plan (IDP)

This tool helps leaders and team members co-create meaningful development conversations.

Instructions:

1. Start with recent performance feedback and key organizational competencies.

2. Identify two core strengths and two growth areas for each team member.

3. Team members should complete the plan independently and then align with their leader.

4. Ask:

   ○ How have I accomplished my biggest wins?

   ○ What feedback do I consistently receive, and how can I grow from it?

5. Select on-the-job actions to support development. Link growth goals to measurable impact.

Meet & Greet Form

Build trust and connection from the start. Use this form when joining a new team or welcoming new hires.

Instructions:

- Block at least 2 hours for this conversation; don't rush it.

- Use the prompts to guide a mutual exchange: both leader and team member should share.

- Focus on values, motivations, work styles, and communication preferences.

This is not a checklist; it's a relationship-building moment.

Rules of Engagement – Team Example

These are the behavioral standards your team agrees to live by, especially during high-stakes conversations, decision-making, and shared work.

Instructions:

- Use the acronym RESPECT or your own acronym. Each letter represents a behavior you all commit to.

- Post your agreed-upon rules where the team can revisit them regularly.

- Return to them when things get tense; they're a reset, not a one-time activity.

A high-accountability culture is not just upheld by leaders; it's reinforced by peers.

Development & Feedback Escalation Map

Most leaders escalate too soon (reactive) or too late (avoidant). This tool helps you strike the right balance.

Instructions:

- Use this map to identify when to:

  - Coach

  - Reset expectations

  - Escalate with support

- Use specific actions to move behavior forward, not just

monitor it.

Escalation should feel fair, predictable, and rooted in development, not surprise or emotion.

5 Cs Courageous Conversation Planner

Coach Quen's framework for accountability conversations that are direct, respectful, and effective.

Instructions:

- Use this planner to prepare for any difficult conversation.

- Reflect on and write out each of the 5 Cs:

  - **Clarity** – What's the issue?

  - **Candor** – What needs to be said directly?

  - **Curiosity** – What do I need to ask or understand?

  - **Credibility** – How will I model the standard?

  - **Consistency** – What happens next?

This tool helps you stay focused, emotionally grounded, and impactful in the moment.

Chapter Twelve

About Dr. Quendrida Whitmore

Quendrida loves leadership! Her passion for people inspired her to launch Quendrida Whitmore Coaching & Consulting, where, as Coach Quen®, she helps leaders and organizations transform their futures. Quendrida has a passion for empowering great teams to drive excellent results. Her ability to identify culture gaps and infuse alignment is where she thrives. Coach Quen facilitates increased trust among groups to create a cohesive, high-performing team. Additionally, she enjoys helping individuals accomplish life-changing personal goals, authentically believing in development for all.

Quendrida gained experience in executive positions, leading teams for over 25 years. Her leadership started with Target Corporation in various areas of the organization, specifically as a buyer in merchandising, director in loss prevention, and senior director in operations. Subsequently, she went on to Ross Stores, where she was promoted to regional vice president of operations. Her career then led her to a senior vice president in hospitality and operations with WeWork as Head of Community in the United States, Canada, Peru, and Costa Rica.

Quendrida received her master's in business administration and is a certified coach, earning her CPCC from Co-Active Training Institute. She also received her EdD from the University of Southern California with a focus on Organizational Change and Leadership.

My vision is "to rid the world of bad bosses!"[TM] – Coach Quen

About Quendrida Whitmore Coaching & Consulting

Coach Quen is dedicated to empowering individuals and organizations to achieve their fullest potential through transformative coaching and leadership development programs.

Our mission is to foster an environment of growth and innovation, where diverse talents are nurtured and turned into dynamic leadership capabilities, ensuring that every client cannot only meet but exceed their personal and professional goals. We strive to create a more inclusive and equitable world, one leader at a time.

Our Services:

- **Leadership Workshops:** Group and organizational training to help transform teams.

- **Team Building & Org Agility:** Leverage individual strengths, build trust, and set goals for success.

- **Executive Coaching:** One-on-one coaching to help you realize your life's purpose.

- **Career Coaching:** Guidance, consulting & mentoring on your current career or a new one.

- **Speaker & Panelist:** Need a dynamic and experienced speaker? Book Coach Quen®!

Core Values

- **Self-awareness:** Encouraging a deep understanding of one's strengths, weaknesses, emotions, and motivations. This awareness enables individuals to lead with authenticity, make informed decisions, and foster meaningful relationships in personal and professional settings.

- **Empowerment:** Facilitating personal and professional growth to enable individuals and organizations to reach their fullest potential.

- **Innovation:** Promoting creative solutions and continuous improvement in leadership practices.

- **Diversity and Inclusion:** Building an inclusive environment where diverse talents are nurtured into dynamic leadership capabilities.

- **Commitment and Involvement:** Creating a sense of commitment and involvement through purpose-driven actions and decisions. Intentional actions.

Visit us at CoachQuen.com to learn more!